THE SCIENCE OF
SOUND

PROJECTS AND EXPERIMENTS
WITH MUSIC AND SOUND WAVES

Bibliographical Note

TABLETOP SCIENTIST: THE SCIENCE OF SOUND, Projects and Experiments with Music and Sound Waves, first published by Dover Publications, Inc., in 2013, is an unabridged reprint of the work originally produced by David West Children's Books, London, in 2005. Minor corrections have been made to the text.

International Standard Book Number

ISBN-13: 978-0-486-49263-6
ISBN-10: 0-486-49263-X

Manufactured in China
49263X01
www.doverpublications.com

TABLETOP SCIENTIST: THE SCIENCE OF SOUND
was produced by

David West 🧑‍🤝‍🧑 Children's Books
7 Princeton Court
55 Felsham Road
London SW15 1AZ

Designer: David West
Editor: Gail Bushnell
Picture Research: Gail Bushnell

PHOTO CREDITS :
Abbreviations: t-top, m-middle, b-bottom, r-right,
l-left, c-centre.

Pages 6, 8, 12, 16, 20tl – Corbis Images. 20tr – Corel. 4t, 26 (CSU Archive/Everett) – Rex Features Ltd.

Every effort has been made to contact copyright holders of any material reproduced in this book. Any omissions will be rectified in subsequent printings if notice is given to the publishers.

With special thanks to the models: Meshach Burton, Sam Heming De-Allie, Annabel Garnham, Andrew Gregson, Hannah Holmes, Molly Rose Ibbett, Margaux Monfared, Max Monfared, Charlotte Moore, Beth Shon, Meg Shon, William Slater, Danielle Smale and Pippa Stannard.

An explanation of difficult words can be found in the glossary on page 31.

THE SCIENCE OF
SOUND

PROJECTS AND EXPERIMENTS
WITH MUSIC AND SOUND WAVES

STEVE PARKER

DOVER PUBLICATIONS, INC.
Mineola, New York

TABLETOP SCIENTIST

CONTENTS

From early
telephones…

…to soundproof
studios to…

…breaking the
sound barrier, the
technology of sound
moves ahead at
tremendous speed.

INTRODUCTION

The only silent place is deep in space. On Earth there are always faint sounds. Some sounds are too tiny for our ears, but scientific devices and some animals can detect them. Sounds play a huge part in our lives from talking and listening to the radio to the annoying noise of road traffic. Sounds also play a vital role in science and technology. The science of sound is known as acoustics. It has allowed engineers to build machines that use sounds to shatter rocks, measure distances accurately, and see inside our bodies. All of these topics and processes and many more rely on our knowledge of the science of sound.

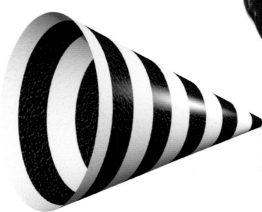

HOW IT WORKS

These panels explain the scientific ideas in each project and the processes that make it work.

Prepare each project carefully and follow the instructions. Remember: real scientists always put safety first.

Where you see these symbols:

 Ask an adult to help you.

 Project to be done outdoors.

 Sharp tools may be needed.

 Prepare work surface for a messy project.

TRY IT AND SEE

These panels show more ideas to try so you can experiment and find out more about sound.

5

WHAT IS SOUND?

Sound is movement. It's a special kind of back and forth movement called vibration. Objects that vibrate many times each second send out sounds. These travel as "sound waves" through the air. The waves are movements of tiny particles called atoms and molecules which make up air. You cannot see sound waves but sometimes you can feel them.

Space is silent, because there is no air (or anything else) to vibrate and carry sound waves.

PROJECT: MAKE A SOUND CANNON

SOUND CANNON

WHAT YOU NEED

- balloon
- large cardboard tube
- cardboard
- tape
- glue
- wooden spoon or stick

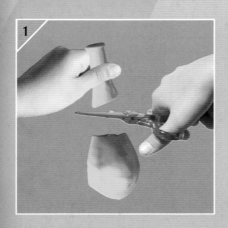

CAREFULLY CUT THE NECK OFF THE BALLOON. A LARGE, ROUND PARTY BALLOON IS BEST FOR THIS PROJECT.

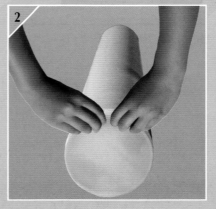

STRETCH THE BALLOON OVER ONE END OF THE LARGE CARDBOARD TUBE SO IT IS FAIRLY TAUT. TAPE IT FIRMLY AROUND THE EDGES.

BEND THE CARDBOARD INTO A CONE SHAPE AND TAPE ALONG THE EDGE. TRIM THE ENDS WITH SCISSORS, LEAVING A THUMB-SIZED HOLE AT THE NARROW END.

THE POWER OF SOUND WAVES

Sound waves have alternating areas of high air pressure and low air pressure. In high pressure areas, the tiny particles in air are closer together.

In low air pressure areas, the particles are farther apart. The cone funnels them together, increasing pressure.

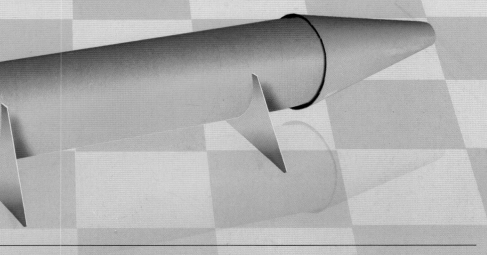

SOUND WAVES PRESSURE INCREASES

VIBRATING BALLOON CREATES SOUND WAVES

SOUND WAVES TRAVEL THROUGH AIR

BANG!

CUT OUT CARDBOARD TARGETS AND STAND THEM IN FRONT OF THE CANNON. GIVE A SHORT, SHARP HIT TO THE STRETCHED BALLOON WITH THE STICK. SOUND WAVES "SHOOT" OUT OF THE HOLE AND THEIR PRESSURE KNOCKS OVER THE TARGETS. HOW FAR AWAY CAN YOU KNOCK THEM OVER?

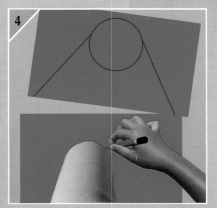

4

MAKE SOME STANDS OUT OF THE CARDBOARD. DRAW AROUND THE TUBE AS SHOWN SO THAT IT WILL FIT INTO EACH STAND, AND CUT OUT THE STANDS CAREFULLY.

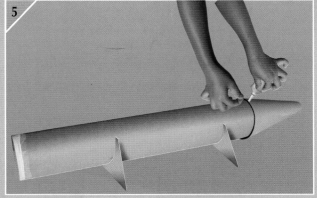

5

GLUE OR TAPE THE STANDS TO THE TUBE. THEN GLUE OR TAPE THE CONE TO THE TUBE AT THE OPPOSITE END TO THE BALLOON. THE TUBE SHOULD REST FIRMLY ON ITS STANDS. (YOU MAY WANT TO ADD EXTRA STANDS.)

TRY IT

Change the sound cannon so it has a balloon skin over each end. Hold it upright and put some small objects like beads on the top. What happens to them if you tap the lower balloon skin?

SOUNDS UNDERWATER

Sounds are vibrations of the tiny particles that make up substances. We usually hear sound waves that pass through air. But many other substances carry sounds too. These substances are known as sound media and include liquids like water and solids such as woods, metals, and plastics.

A submarine sends out "pings" of sound to hear if they bounce off nearby objects. This is called echo-sounding or sonar.

Dolphins "talk" underwater using clicks, squeals, grunts, and many other noises. Sounds travel more than four times faster through water than through air.

PROJECT: EXPERIMENT WITH SOUNDS IN WATER AND OTHER MATERIALS

SOUNDS IN WATER

WHAT YOU NEED

- large fish tank
- paper or plastic cups
- straw

HMM, BLIP, PING, CLICK
HOLD A PLASTIC CUP ON THE SIDE OF THE TANK WITH ITS BASE FLAT AGAINST THE GLASS AND YOUR EAR IN THE OPEN END. YOUR HELPER PLACES THE STRAW INTO THE WATER AND MAKES NOISES INTO IT, SUCH AS HUMMING. TRY HUMS AT DIFFERENT VOLUMES, AND FROM HIGH PITCH TO LOW.

THE BEST TYPE OF TANK FOR THIS PROJECT IS ONE WITH FLAT GLASS SIDES. (DON'T USE A TANK WITH FISH IN IT. IT COULD SERIOUSLY HURT THEM!)

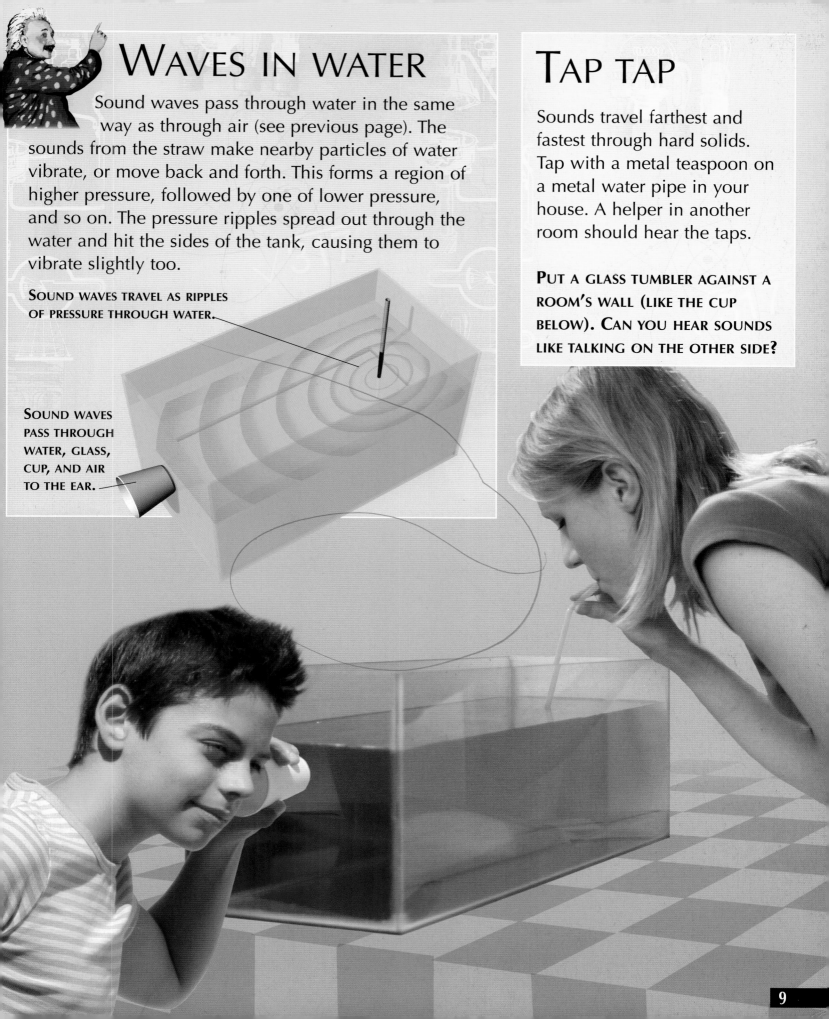

WAVES IN WATER

Sound waves pass through water in the same way as through air (see previous page). The sounds from the straw make nearby particles of water vibrate, or move back and forth. This forms a region of higher pressure, followed by one of lower pressure, and so on. The pressure ripples spread out through the water and hit the sides of the tank, causing them to vibrate slightly too.

SOUND WAVES TRAVEL AS RIPPLES
OF PRESSURE THROUGH WATER.

SOUND WAVES
PASS THROUGH
WATER, GLASS,
CUP, AND AIR
TO THE EAR.

TAP TAP

Sounds travel farthest and fastest through hard solids. Tap with a metal teaspoon on a metal water pipe in your house. A helper in another room should hear the taps.

PUT A GLASS TUMBLER AGAINST A ROOM'S WALL (LIKE THE CUP BELOW). CAN YOU HEAR SOUNDS LIKE TALKING ON THE OTHER SIDE?

QUIET ... OR ... LOUD!

What's the difference between a whisper and a shout? The latter is louder! One of sound's main features is its volume or loudness. This is a measure of the energy that the sound waves contain. The bigger an object's vibrations, the louder the sound or noise.

An acoustic guitar's hollow body acts as a soundbox.

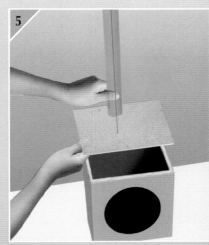

PROJECT: MAKE A TWANGER—MAKE IT LOUDER

TWANGER

WHAT YOU NEED

- **cardboard box**
- **cardboard tube or dowel**
- **small sheet of plywood**
- **string**
- **glue**
- **scissors**

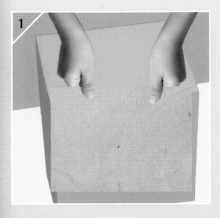

CUT A SQUARE OF THIN PLYWOOD TO THE SAME SIZE AS ONE SIDE OF THE BOX. MAKE A SMALL HOLE IN THE CENTER OF THE SHEET.

GLUE THE CARDBOARD TUBE SECURELY TO THE PLYWOOD, PLACING IT HALFWAY ALONG ONE SIDE AND NEAR THE EDGE. CAREFULLY MAKE A SMALL SLIT IN THE TOP OF THE TUBE ON THE SIDE NEAREST THE HOLE. TIE A LARGE KNOT AT ONE END OF THE STRING. THREAD THE OTHER END UP THROUGH THE HOLE. PULL THE STRING THROUGH AND SLIDE THE UPPER END INTO THE SLIT, SO THE STRING IS HELD FIRMLY, STRETCHED, AND TAUT.

NOW TWANG THE STRING. HOW LOUD IS IT?

CAREFULLY CUT OUT THE SIDE OF THE BOX, BUT LEAVE A NARROW STRIP ALL AROUND.

WITH THE SQUARE CUT-OUT ON TOP, CAREFULLY TRIM OUT A CIRCLE FROM THE FRONT.

GLUE THE PLYWOOD SHEET TO THE EDGE AROUND THE TOP OF THE BOX AND ALLOW TO DRY.

TALL = LOUD

With the plywood sheet on the table and no soundbox, only the string vibrates. This makes a quiet sound. Add the soundbox, and the plywood sheet can now vibrate easily. It passes its movements to the box and the air inside, so these vibrate too. The sound is much louder. If you imagine sound waves as up-and-down lines, then the line's height or amplitude shows the volume.

SOUND WAVES BOUNCE AROUND INSIDE BOX AND SET IT VIBRATING

QUIET SOUND HAS LOW WAVES

LOUD SOUND HAS HIGH WAVES

A LOUDER SOUND

NOW TWANG THE STRING AGAIN. COMPARE IT TO THE VOLUME OF THE SOUND EARLIER, WITHOUT THE BOX (STEP 2). ITS SOUND SHOULD BE MUCH LOUDER. THE BOX WORKS AS AN ACOUSTIC AMPLIFIER, AS EXPLAINED ABOVE. WHAT HAPPENS IF YOU DRAPE A CLOTH OVER THE CIRCULAR HOLE?

PLAY IT AGAIN

The twanger's volume depends partly on how hard you pluck the string. A harder twang makes it vibrate more, so it is louder. Try making a twanger with a smaller soundbox. What happens?

TRY PULLING THE TUBE TOP TO TIGHTEN THE STRING AS YOU TWANG—THEN SEE NEXT PAGE.

HIGH OR LOW

Some sounds are very low or deep, like thunder and jet engines. Others are high or shrill, like squeals and singing birds. This feature of sound is called pitch. It depends on how many vibrations or waves there are each second. This is known as sound's frequency.

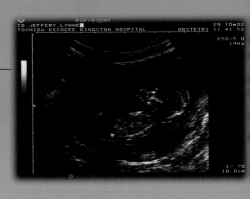

Very high-pitched sounds, called ultrasound, reflect off parts inside the body —like this baby in the body.

Elephants "talk" in rumbles so deep we cannot hear them.

PROJECT: BUILD A BOTTLE XYLOPHONE

BOTTLE XYLOPHONE

1

POUR WATER INTO EACH GLASS BOTTLE OR JAR. ADD MORE WATER TO EACH ONE SO THE FIRST ONE IS NEARLY EMPTY AND THE LAST ONE IS ALMOST FULL. PLACE THE BOTTLES OR JARS IN A ROW ON THE TABLE.

WHAT YOU NEED

- **eight similar glass bottles or jars**
- **water**
- **wooden spoon or stick**

TUNE THE XYLOPHONE
GENTLY TAP THE BOTTLES. THE SOUND CHANGES GETTING HIGHER IN PITCH FROM THE EMPTIEST BOTTLE TO THE FULLEST. ADD OR REMOVE WATER TO EACH AS NECESSARY TO MAKE THE NOTES OF THE MUSICAL SCALE: DOH, RAY, ME, FA, SO, LA, TEE, DOH. NOW YOU'RE READY TO PLAY A TUNE!

SHORTER = HIGHER

When you tap a bottle, it and the air inside vibrate. The emptiest bottle has the most air, and vibrates slowest. It makes long sound waves with a low pitch.

This bottle has a low frequency (number of waves each second). The fullest bottle has the least air. This vibrates fastest and produces the highest pitch or frequency.

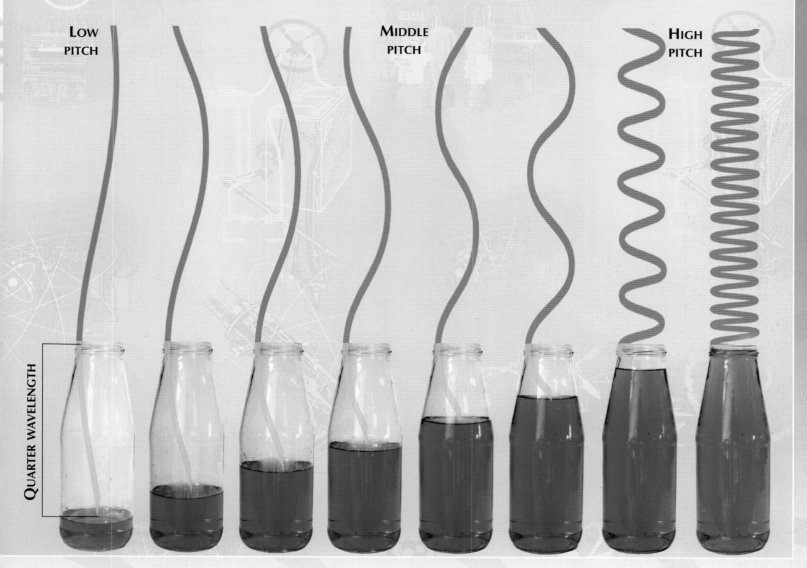

LOW PITCH

MIDDLE PITCH

HIGH PITCH

QUARTER WAVELENGTH

HUMMING GLASS

Rub a wet finger gently around the rim of a glass held by its stem. Can you hear a hum?

DOES THE PITCH CHANGE IF YOU PUT MORE LIQUID INTO THE GLASS?

HEARING SOUNDS

Sound waves get trapped in a hollow object like a vase or shell. Held close to the ear, we hear them jumbled up, and they sound like the sea.

Our ears work by changing sound vibrations into nerve signals. Sound waves travel through skin, bone, water, and hairs inside the ear as vibrations. These vibrations are then made into nerve signals that carry a message to the brain which identifies the sound.

PROJECT: BUILD A MODEL EAR

MODEL EAR

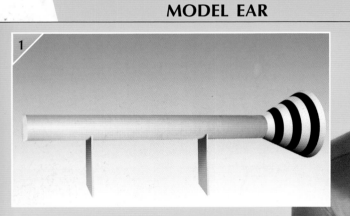

MAKE A SOUND CANNON AS SHOWN ON PAGES 6-7. FIX THE CONE WITH THE NARROW END POINTING INTO THE TUBE, AS SHOWN ABOVE.

TAPE A STRAW TO THE CENTER OF THE BALLOON. SET UP THE TUBE SO THE END OF THE STRAW JUST POKES INTO THE SURFACE OF WATER IN A BOWL. THE SOUND CANNON IS NOW READY TO BECOME AN EAR!

WHAT YOU NEED

- **balloon**
- **large cardboard tube**
- **cardboard**
- **tape**
- **glue**
- **wooden spoon or stick**
- **bowl of water**
- **straw**

HEAR EAR

Sound waves travel along the tube-shaped ear canal and vibrate a thin, stretched bit of skin called the eardrum. This sends vibrations along three tiny bones, called the hammer, anvil, and stirrup. The stirrup sends the vibrations into a fluid inside the snail-shaped cochlea. They cause ripples which shake microscopic hairs inside and these send nerve signals to the brain.

SEE THE SOUND

A HELPER HITS A BOX WITH A STICK. THE SOUND VIBRATIONS PASS THROUGH THE AIR AND ARE FUNNELED INTO THE TUBE LIKE SOUNDS PASSING INTO YOUR EAR CANAL. THE WAVES THEN HIT THE BALLOON, WHICH VIBRATES LIKE YOUR EARDRUM. NEXT, THE VIBRATIONS PASS ALONG THE STRAW JUST AS THEY DO ALONG YOUR EAR BONES. THE VIBRATIONS CAUSE THE RIPPLES YOU CAN SEE IN THE WATER.

COCHLEA (= BOWL OF WATER)

EAR BONES (= STRAW)

SOUND WAVES

NERVE TO BRAIN

EARDRUM (= BALLOON)

EAR CANAL (= TUBE)

OUTER EAR (= CONE)

Owls use stereo hearing to locate prey.

WHERE'S THAT SOUND?

Close your eyes and listen and you can probably tell whether a sound comes from the left, right, front or back. This is because you have two ears! They face opposite directions, and are several inches apart. So each ear picks up slightly different sounds, that your brain automatically compares. This is called stereophonic hearing or "stereo" for short.

Patented in 1880, this device helped ships' captains work out the direction of a ship's horn in thick fog.

PROJECT: THE STEREO DIRECTION FINDER

STEREO DIRECTION FINDER

WHAT YOU NEED

- **2 large sheets of paper**
- **six feet of soft plastic tube (1/2 inch diameter)**
- **tape**
- **radio**
- **scissors**
- **blindfold**
- **plastic cups**

MAKE A FUNNEL AS SHOWN ON PAGE 22. TAPE 3 FEET OF TUBE TO THE END. MAKE TWO OF THESE.

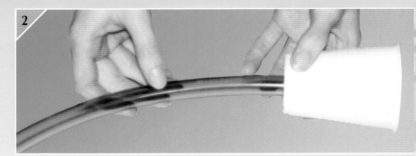

CUT A HOLE IN THE BOTTOM OF A PLASTIC CUP. INSERT THE OTHER END OF THE TUBE INTO IT TO CHECK IT FITS. DO NOT GLUE THE TUBE TO THE CUPS YET.

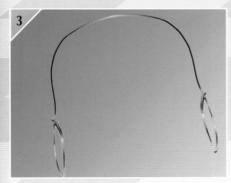

BEND THE WIRE AROUND YOUR HEAD. BEND TWO LOOPS AT THE ENDS TO ALIGN WITH YOUR EARS.

FIT THE PLASTIC CUPS THROUGH THE WIRE LOOPS. GLUE OR TAPE THE TUBES TO THE CUPS. PUT THE "HEADPHONES" ON YOUR HEAD SO THE CUPS FIT OVER YOUR EARS.

LOUDER, SOONER

Because of sound's speed (see next page), noises reach one ear before the other. The difference is less than 1/1,000th of a second, but the brain knows. Sound also fades and the brain detects it is louder in the nearer ear. When sounds are equal in both ears, you are facing the source.

SOUND IN FARTHER EAR IS LATER AND QUIETER

SOUND IN NEARER EAR IS SOONER AND LOUDER

FACE THE MUSIC
GET YOUR HELPER TO PUT ON YOUR BLINDFOLD. YOU HOLD THE FUNNEL FACING FORWARD AT ARMS' LENGTH. YOUR HELPER QUIETLY MOVES TO AN UNKNOWN SPOT AND HOLDS A RADIO AT LOW VOLUME. YOU THEN USE THE DIRECTION FINDER TO LOCATE THE SOUND.

REPEAT THE EXPERIMENT WITHOUT THE DIRECTION FINDER BUT WITH THE BLINDFOLD ON. WHICH IS EASIER?

BEHIND YOU!

Try moving the funnels in different directions like a rabbit moving its ears separately. Does this help to locate the sound source?

SEE WHAT HAPPENS WHEN YOU:
• CHANGE THE TUBES SO THEY GO TO OPPOSITE EARS.
• TURN THE FUNNELS TO FACE BACKWARD!

SPEED OF SOUND

Sounds do not travel instantly. They take time, in the world of science, quite a long time. Sound waves travel through air at about 1100 feet per second (760 miles per hour), depending on conditions. Objects moving faster than this, like bullets and jet fighters, are said to be supersonic.

The first passenger plane to fly faster than sound was the Russian-built Tu-144 on 5 June 1969. But unlike its similar rival Concorde, the Tu-144 never went into regular service.

The first supersonic person was Chuck Yeager who flew in the Bell X-1 plane, in 1947.

PROJECT: SHOW HOW SLOW SOUND IS

YOUR HELPER WALKS A LONG WAY AWAY (100–200 YARDS). WHEN YOU ARE READY WITH THE STOPWATCH, GIVE A SIGNAL. THE HELPER PRICKS THE BALLOON WITH A PIN. WHEN YOU SEE THE PUFF OF BABY POWDER AS THE BALLOON BURSTS, IMMEDIATELY START THE WATCH.

SHOW HOW SLOW SOUND IS

USING A PAPER FUNNEL, POUR SEVERAL SPOONFULS OF BABY POWDER INTO A LARGE PARTY BALLOON.

BLOW UP THE BALLOON AND TIE IT AT THE NECK. TAKE IT AND THE STOPWATCH TO AN OPEN, SAFE, QUIET PLACE.

1

2

WHAT YOU NEED

- balloon
- baby powder
- stopwatch
- paper
- spoon
- pin

SOUND WAVES AS CAR APPROACHES ARE CLOSER TOGETHER AND LISTENER HEARS HIGHER PITCH

DOPPLER EFFECT

A moving sound source travels forward slightly between sending out each sound wave, so the waves in front bunch together with a higher frequency. The opposite happens behind. This makes the "neeeowww" sound.

SOUND WAVES AS CAR PASSES ARE FARTHER APART AND LISTENER HEARS LOWER PITCH

WARNING: STAND CLEAR OF THE ROAD. DO NOT STEP INTO THE ROAD.

NOTE
YOU NEED A QUIET PLACE AND CALM, CLEAR CONDITIONS FOR THIS PROJECT, OTHERWISE THE SOUND WILL NOT CARRY FAR ENOUGH.

FLASH...BANG!
VERY QUICKLY AFTER THE PUFF OF POWDER, YOU SHOULD HEAR THE BANG OF THE BALLOON BURSTING. BE READY FOR THIS, AND STOP THE WATCH AS SOON AS YOU HEAR THE BANG. CHECK THE TIME ON THE WATCH. IF YOU ARE 340 YARDS AWAY FROM YOUR HELPER, THEN SOUND TRAVELS THIS FAR IN EXACTLY ONE SECOND. IF THE TIME IS LESS OR MORE, TRY WORKING OUT THE DISTANCE OF YOUR HELPER.

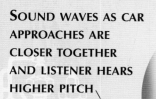

SOUND VS LIGHT

Light travels so fast that the waves from the powder burst reach your eyes almost instantly. Sound waves go one million times slower, which is why you hear the burst later.

LIGHT (982 MILLION FEET PER SECOND)

SOUND (340 YARDS PER SECOND)

BOUNCING SOUND

The hard rock of cliffs and canyons produces clear echoes with long time delays.

In a mirror, we see light rays that bounce or reflect off it. When sound waves hit a hard, smooth surface, they also reflect off it. This happens when we shout at a hard surface faraway like a wall or cliff. We hear the sound returning after a time gap. This reflection is an echo.

Bats listen to the reflection of their squeaks off nearby objects, to find their way in the dark.

PROJECT: EXPERIMENT WITH REFLECTED SOUND

REFLECTED SOUND

WHAT YOU NEED

- **cardboard**
- **egg cartons**
- **clock or radio**
- **blindfold**
- **glue**
- **scissors**

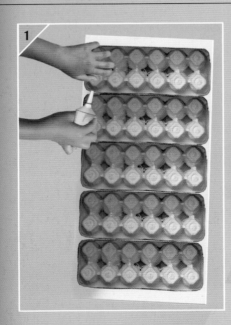

1 CAREFULLY CUT THE LIDS OFF THE EGG CARTONS. GLUE THE BOTTOM PARTS, WHERE THE EGGS SIT, ONTO A BIG SHEET OF STIFF CARDBOARD TO MAKE A SOUND BAFFLE.

2 CUT FOUR TRIANGLES FROM CARDBOARD, FOR STANDS. GLUE TWO OF THESE TO THE SOUND BAFFLE AND TWO TO ANOTHER PLAIN CARDBOARD SHEET.

SET UP THE SOUND BAFFLE NEAR THE EDGE OF A TABLE, CARTONS FACING INWARD. PLACE THE PLAIN CARDBOARD AT THE OPPOSITE CORNER, AT AN ANGLE OF 45°.

REFLECTIONS

The two cards affect sound waves in different ways. The soft, lumpy surface of the sound baffle reflects waves poorly and jumbles them up (see pages 24–25) so they can hardly be heard on the other side. The plain card works like a "sound mirror" and reflects waves well so they seem to be coming straight from it.

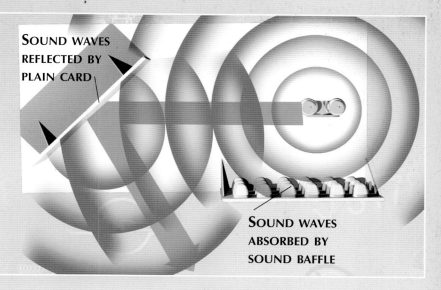

SOUND WAVES REFLECTED BY PLAIN CARD

SOUND WAVES ABSORBED BY SOUND BAFFLE

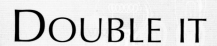

HEARING REFLECTIONS

YOUR HELPER BLINDFOLDS YOU AND SPINS YOU AROUND TWO OR THREE TIMES. THEN THE HELPER PLACES A LOUDLY TICKING CLOCK, OR A SMALL RADIO SET TO LOW VOLUME, NEAR THE END OF THE TABLE AWAY FROM THE PLAIN CARD. YOU LISTEN CAREFULLY AND POINT TO THE DIRECTION OF THE SOUND. WITH THE BLINDFOLD REMOVED, YOU SEE THAT YOU HAVE PROBABLY POINTED TO THE REFLECTING CARD.

TRY CHANGING THE ANGLE OF THE REFLECTING CARD. DOES THIS CHANGE THE PLACE WHERE YOU HEAR THE CLOCK OR RADIO LOUDEST?

DOUBLE IT

Try making two reflecting cards and position them on either side. Where does the sound seem to come from now?

Our voice-box (larynx) holds two vibrating strips—vocal cords.

MAKING SOUNDS

A clarinet's reed is in the mouthpiece. The keys alter the note or pitch.

Many devices are designed to vibrate and produce sounds from loudspeaker cones, drum heads, and guitar strings, to our own vocal cords. One common design for making sounds is a thin, slightly flexible strip called a reed. It is used in reed instruments such as clarinets to make the original sounds which are then altered by the main body of the instrument.

PROJECT: BUILD A PARTY HORN

PARTY HORN

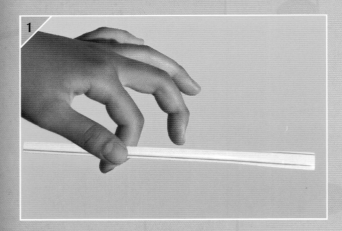

FLATTEN ONE END OF A PLASTIC DRINKING STRAW BY PRESSING AND SLIDING A RULER ALONG IT.

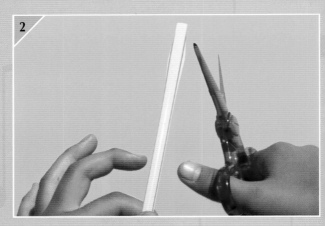

CAREFULLY TRIM THE FLATTENED END ON EITHER SIDE WITH SCISSORS TO MAKE A V-SHAPED REED.

WHAT YOU NEED

- plastic straw
- cardboard
- tape
- glue
- scissors
- compass
- ruler
- pencil

DRAW A CIRCLE ON THE CARDBOARD WITH A COMPASS AND CUT IT OUT. CUT OUT A SECTION OF THE CIRCLE AND A SMALL HOLE IN THE MIDDLE.

TAPE THE EDGES OF THE SHEET TO FORM A FUNNEL. POKE THE FREE END OF THE STRAW JUST INTO THE NARROW END AND TAPE IT FIRMLY.

GOOD VIBRATIONS

As you blow air through the narrow gap between the two strips of the straw end, you make them shake or vibrate.

The movements pass to the rest of the straw and the air inside it, which also vibrate to make the sound louder.

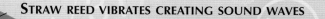

STRAW REED VIBRATES CREATING SOUND WAVES **SOUND WAVES INSIDE STRAW**

AIR

The cone shape on the end of the horn works like a trumpet to make the sound waves pass out as a narrow "beam."

WAAAAH!
PRACTICE BLOWING INTO THE STRAW TO MAKE THE REED VIBRATE. A FEW TIPS:
• MAKE SURE YOUR MOUTH COVERS THE WHOLE REED.
• DON'T HOLD THE REED ITSELF IN YOUR TEETH OR LIPS. LET IT VIBRATE FREELY.
• TRY BLOWING SOFTLY OR SLIGHTLY HARDER.

PERSEVERE AND YOU SHOULD SOON PRODUCE A REEDY, WEEDY, WAILING SOUND!

LONG OR SHORT

Try straws of different length in the horn. Does the sound seem different?

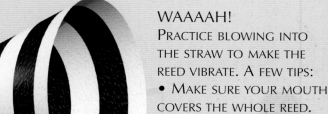

HOLE

WHAT HAPPENS IF YOU MAKE A SMALL HOLE IN THE TOP OF THE STRAW? WHEN YOU BLOW, COVER THE HOLE WITH A FINGER, THEN TAKE AWAY THE FINGER. DOES THE PITCH CHANGE? (SEE PAGES 12–13.)

SOAKING UP SOUND

Sometimes we want to get rid of sound, especially the irritating loud noise of machines, traffic, planes or unwanted music. Substances which absorb or "soak up" sound waves are known as soundproofing materials. Most of them are fairly soft and flexible, with a lumpy or fluffy surface. They change the energy in the sound waves into tiny movements and amounts of heat within their own structure.

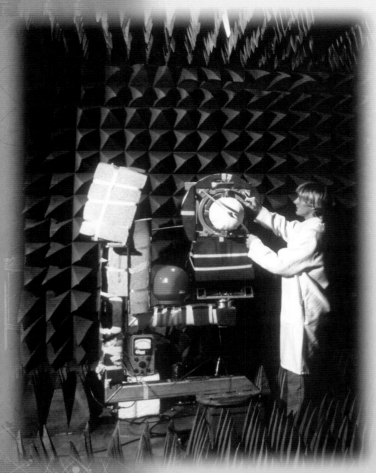

Special soundproofed rooms are used for scientific tests. Foam points cut out reflections from the walls, floor, and ceiling.

PROJECT: BUILD A SOUNDPROOF BOX

SOUNDPROOF BOX

WHAT YOU NEED

- **large cardboard box**
- **egg cartons**
- **glue**
- **scissors**
- **alarm clock**
- **radio**

1

EGG CARTONS MADE OF CARDBOARD RATHER THAN PLASTIC ARE BEST FOR THIS PROJECT. CAREFULLY CUT OFF THE LIDS TO LEAVE THE BASES THAT HOLD THE EGGS.

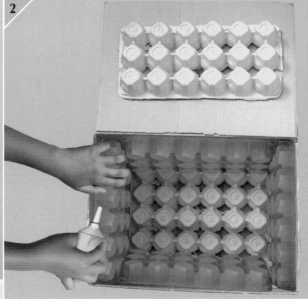

2

GLUE THE BASES ONTO THE INSIDE OF THE CARDBOARD BOX ON THE BOTTOM AND SIDES. WHEN YOU GLUE THEM TO THE LID, LEAVE A GAP AROUND THE EDGES SO THE LID FITS SNUGLY.

SOUNDS TO SILENCE

SET AN ALARM CLOCK RINGING AND PUT IT INTO THE SOUNDPROOF BOX. CLOSE THE LID. CAN YOU STILL HEAR IT? TRY PUTTING A SMALL RADIO INTO THE BOX. VARY THE VOLUME UNTIL YOU CANNOT HEAR IT AT ALL WHEN IT IS INSIDE. NOTE THE VOLUME LEVEL ON THE KNOB OR DIAL. NOW EXPERIMENT WITH OTHER SOUNDPROOFING MATERIALS SUGGESTED BELOW. CHANGE THE VOLUME LEVEL ON THE RADIO IN THE SAME WAY UNTIL IT CANNOT BE HEARD INSIDE THE BOX. WHICH MATERIAL CUTS OUT THE HIGHEST VOLUME LEVEL ON THE RADIO AND SO IS THE BEST SOUNDPROOFER?

ABSORBED ENERGY

As sound waves hit the soundproofing material, some are absorbed into it and their energy is changed into other forms. Other waves are reflected, jumbled, and scattered at random and are too weak to hear.

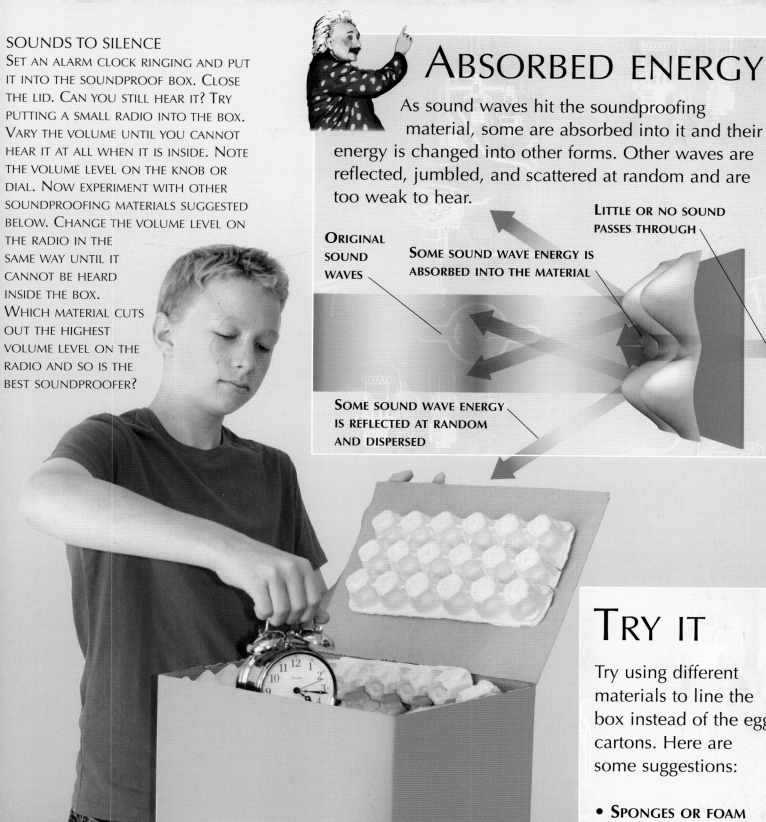

LITTLE OR NO SOUND PASSES THROUGH

ORIGINAL SOUND WAVES

SOME SOUND WAVE ENERGY IS ABSORBED INTO THE MATERIAL

SOME SOUND WAVE ENERGY IS REFLECTED AT RANDOM AND DISPERSED

TRY IT

Try using different materials to line the box instead of the egg cartons. Here are some suggestions:

- **SPONGES OR FOAM PLASTIC/RUBBER**
- **NEWSPAPER CRUSHED INTO SMALL BALLS**
- **COTTON BALLS**
- **PIECES OF OLD CARPET**

SOUND ALONG A LINE

Alexander Graham Bell invented the telephone in 1876. Here he opens the New York-to-Chicago line in 1892.

Real telephones change sounds into patterns of electrical signals or laser light flashes that can be sent long distances along cables. But sounds can also travel considerable distances along certain substances, as shown earlier in the book. One such substance is ordinary string!

PROJECT: MAKE A PAPER CUP TELEPHONE

PAPER CUP TELEPHONE

1

CAREFULLY MAKE A SMALL HOLE IN THE BOTTOM OF EACH CUP WITH A SHARP PENCIL.

2

THREAD THE STRING THROUGH EACH HOLE AND TIE A LARGE KNOT AT EACH END.

WHAT YOU NEED

- paper or plastic cups
- 12 to 30 feet of string
- sharp pencil

SEND AND RECEIVE

When you speak into the cup, the sound waves of your voice make the cup itself vibrate, especially at its base. (A diaphragm is a thin sheet that vibrates like this and is used in most microphones.)

The vibrations then travel along the taut string. At the other cup the reverse happens. The paper cup's base is like a loudspeaker diaphragm or cone vibrating to send sounds into the ear.

VIBRATIONS FROM STRING MAKE CUP BASE VIBRATE

SOUND WAVES MAKE CUP BASE VIBRATE

VIBRATIONS MAKE SOUND WAVES IN AIR THAT PASS TO EAR

VIBRATIONS TRAVEL ALONG STRING FROM ONE CUP TO THE OTHER

SOUND WAVES FROM MOUTH PASS THROUGH AIR

HELLO, CAN YOU HEAR ME?

YOU AND YOUR HELPER EACH HOLD A CUP, GRIPPING IT LIGHTLY BY THE RIM. THE STRING MUST BE KEPT TAUT. YOU SPEAK INTO YOUR CUP AND YOUR HELPER HOLDS THE CUP TO THE EAR TO HEAR YOUR WORDS. THEN YOU REVERSE THE PROCESS SO YOUR HELPER SPEAKS AND YOU LISTEN.

EXTRA LINE

Try adding a third cup and piece of string tied to the middle of the main string. Can three of you make a "conference call?"

SEE WHAT HAPPENS WHEN YOU:
- **LET THE STRING GO SLACK.**
- **USE DIFFERENT MATERIALS INSTEAD OF STRING, SUCH AS YARN, THREAD OR THIN WIRE.**

RECORDED SOUND

Speech, music, and other sounds consist of thousands of sound waves, of different pitches and volumes. These can be "captured" as electrical signals and then stored in various forms such as grooves in a vinyl record, micropits on a CD, or micro-magnetic patches on tape or disk.

In 1877 Thomas Edison first recorded sound on his "phonograph."

PROJECT: BUILD A RECORD PLAYER

RECORD PLAYER

WARNING! This project will damage the vinyl record. So use a record that is no longer needed or is about to be thrown away.

WHAT YOU NEED

- **cardboard box**
- **paper**
- **drinking straw**
- **thick & thin cardboard**
- **glue**
- **scissors**
- **tape**
- **old record**
- **paper or plastic cup**
- **needle**
- **pencil**
- **modeling clay**

1

STICK A STRAW ONTO A PIECE OF THICK CARDBOARD. THIS BASE WILL HELP TO HOLD THE STRAW IN POSITION IN THE BOX TOP.

2

MAKE A HOLE SLIGHTLY TO ONE SIDE OF THE BOX TOP, USING A SHARP PENCIL. PUSH THE STRAW THROUGH FROM BENEATH AND GLUE IT AND ITS BASE IN PLACE.

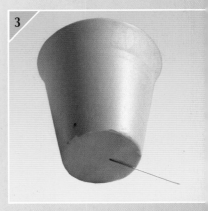

3

CUT THE BOTTOM OUT OF THE CUP. TRIM A CIRCLE OF PAPER TO THE SAME SIZE AND GLUE IT TO THE CUP. TAPE A SEWING NEEDLE TO THE CIRCLE AS SHOWN.

4

PUT THE RECORD ONTO THE BOX, THE STRAW IN ITS CENTER HOLE. CUT A STRIP OF THIN CARDBOARD AND BEND IT IN THE MIDDLE. TAPE ONE END OF THE STRIP TO THE CUP AND THE OTHER TO THE BOX, SO THE NEEDLE IS AT A SLIGHT ANGLE. THE FOLDED CARD WORKS LIKE A SPRING, PRESSING DOWN THE NEEDLE.

5

MAKE A CONE OF THIN PAPER AND GLUE IT TO THE CUP. IF IT OVER-BALANCES THE CUP, PUT MODELING CLAY INTO THE CUP TO KEEP THE NEEDLE PRESSED ONTO THE RECORD.

FOR THE RECORD

GENTLY ROTATE THE RECORD IN THE SAME DIRECTION THAT THE NEEDLE POINTS. (TURNING IT THE WRONG WAY MAKES THE NEEDLE DIG IN.) EXPERIMENT WITH:

• THE SPEED OF ROTATION OF THE RECORD, SLOWER OR FASTER.

• THE PRESSURE OF THE NEEDLE ON THE RECORD, WHICH CAN BE CHANGED BY ADDING OR REMOVING MODELING CLAY IN THE CUP.

GROOVY SOUNDS

Your phonograph works like a real one. As the record's wavy groove passes the needle, it makes the needle vibrate. The movements travel up to a thin flexible diaphragm—in your version, the cup's paper base. This vibrates and sends out sound waves, which the cone directs into the air.

DIAPHRAGM VIBRATES

SOUND WAVES INTO AIR

WAVY GROOVE IN RECORD

STYLUS (NEEDLE) ON ARM

HISTORY OF SOUND

340 B.C.E. In ancient Greece the famous scientist and thinker Aristotle suggested that light and sound passed through the air like waves traveling across the sea. Without air, neither could travel.

60 Ancient Roman scientist Gaius Pliny suggested that the flash of lightning and the boom of thunder in a storm were part of the same event and that we hear the boom after we see the flash because sound is slower than light.

1640 Marin Mersenne tried to measure the speed of sound by comparing the time difference between the flash and bang from a gun fired some distance away. He had no stopwatch but used his pulse rate for timing. His rough answer was 1,500 feet per second.

1654 Otto von Guericke made a vacuum pump to suck all the air from a jar. If a bell was put into the jar, then as the air was removed, the sound of the bell faded. This proved that air (or another substance) was needed to carry sound waves.

1845 Christian Doppler arranged for a steam locomotive to pull a car full of trumpeters at high speed past a group of listeners to demonstrate the Doppler effect.

1876 Alexander Graham Bell invented a way of changing sounds to electrical signals to send along a wire—his "speaking telegraph" is now called the telephone.

1877 Thomas Edison was first to record sounds and play them back, with his early type of phonograph. One of his first recordings was "Mary had a little lamb."

1898 Vlademar Poulsen made the first magnetic recordings of sound, on lengths of wire, an early version of the tape recorder.

1904 Emile Berliner began to mass produce flat discs or "gramophone records," now called vinyl records.

1927 *The Jazz Singer* movie had a soundtrack that followed the pictures—it was the first "talkie."

1947 Charles "Chuck" Yeager was the first person to travel faster than the speed of sound in his Bell X-1 rocket plane.

1969 The English-French Concorde made its first flight. Concordes were the only jetliner to make regular flights at supersonic speeds.

1982–83 Mass production of the first CDs (compact disks) for recorded sound.

GLOSSARY

Acoustics science of sound, its various features, and processes

Amplifier device that makes something larger or more powerful, such as sound waves (acoustic amplifier) or electrical signals (electronic amplifier)

Amplitude "height" of a sound wave, linked to loudness or volume

Cochlea small snail-shaped part deep inside the ear, filled with fluid and tiny hairs. It changes vibrations from sound waves into nerve signals for the brain

Diaphragm thin flexible sheet designed to vibrate when sound waves hit it or to vibrate and make sound waves

Echo sound which has bounced or reflected off a hard surface and returns to the listener so it is heard separately from the original sound

Frequency in sound, the number of waves per second, which is related to its pitch (high or low)

Infrasound sounds too low-pitched for our ears to detect (usually with a frequency of less than 20 sound waves per second)

Media in the science of sound, the substances that carry the vibrations or sound waves, such as air or water

Pitch how high or low a sound is. The pitch of a sound depends on the frequency of the vibrations that are making it

Reed in sound, a small bendy strip designed to vibrate rapidly and make sound waves

Soundproofing using substances and shapes to deflect and soak up any unwanted sounds

Stereo (stereophonic) hearing with two ears, when each ear receives slightly different sound waves, helping you to locate the sound

Supersonic moving faster than the speed of sound

Ultrasound sounds too high-pitched for our ears to detect (usually with a frequency of more than 20,000 sound waves per second)

Vibration type of movement back and forth, from side to side around a central or middle point

Volume how loud a sound is. Volume is linked to the height of the sound waves

INDEX